GREAT EXPLORATIONS

DAVID LIVINGSTONE

Deep in the Heart of Africa

Steven Otfinoski

Marshall Cavendish
Benchmark
New York

Marshall Cavendish Benchmark
99 White Plains Road
Tarrytown, NY 10591-9001
www.marshallcavendish.us

Library of Congress Cataloging-in-Publication Data

Otfinoski, Steven.
David Livingstone : deep in the heart of Africa / by Steven Otfinoski.
p. cm. — (Great explorations)
Summary: "An examination of the life and accomplishments of the explorer
and missionary who traveled southern Africa and was the first European to
reach Victoria Falls"—Provided by publisher.
Includes bibliographical references and index.
ISBN-13: 978-0-7614-2226-6
ISBN-10: 0-7614-2226-9
1. Livingstone, David, 1813-1873—Juvenile literature. 2.
Explorers—Africa, Southern—Biography—Juvenile literature. 3.
Explorers—Scotland—Biography—Juvenile literature. 4. Missionaries,
Medical—Africa, Southern—Biography—Juvenile literature. 5.
Missionaries, Medical—Scotland—Biography—Juvenile literature. I. Title. II. Series.

DT1110.L58O84 2006
916.704'23'092—dc22

2005027930

Photo research by Anne Burns Images
Cover photo: Image Works/Mary Evans Picture Library
Cover inset: Royal Geographic Society

The photographs in this book are used by permission and through the courtesy of: *Corbis:* Stefano
Bianchetti, 5, 42; Corbis, 11; Bettman, 15, 47, 53, 55; Hulton Deutsch Collection, 27; Patrick Ward, 32;
Bojon Breceli, 46; Stapleton Collection, 67; Gideon Mendel, 68. *Image Works:* Mary Evans Picture
Library, 8, 13, 18, 20, 23, 35, 37, 38, 58, 61; SSPL, 21, 49; Ann Ronan Picture Library, 50. *Getty
Images:* 17, 28. *Royal Geographic Society:* 22, 30, 40, 43, 64.

Printed in China
1 3 5 6 4 2

Contents

foreword

Long after the New World had been explored and settled, much of Africa still remained unknown to the outside world. Europeans and Asians had been trading and traveling in Africa for centuries, but their contact with Africans was largely confined to northern Africa and the coastal areas. Most of the interior of the continent remained unexplored by Europeans well into the nineteenth century.

Of all the European explorers and adventurers who ventured into the heart of Africa in the 1800s, none was more celebrated than David Livingstone. A Scottish missionary and doctor of extraordinary courage, determination, and ability, Livingstone was a complicated man. He was as mysterious in many ways as the continent he spent much of his adult life exploring.

A devout Christian missionary, he converted only one person in his forty-year career, a tribal chief. The chief eventually returned to

A missionary turned explorer, David Livingstone crisscrossed
southern and central Africa in the more than three
decades he spent on the continent.

his former religion. A loving husband and father, Livingstone's obsession for exploration at times blinded him to his family's best interests. A brilliant observer and explorer, he was the first European to cross central Africa from east to west. A humanitarian who treated Africans with compassion and kindness, he could not get along with his fellow missionaries and eventually exiled himself from all other Europeans.

Most people know Livingstone as the aged explorer who was "found" by newspaper reporter Henry Stanley in 1871. But Stanley and Livingstone were no Lewis and Clark. While Livingstone had a profound influence on the younger Stanley, the men spent only a few short months together in Africa. Livingstone had already made his mark as an explorer by the time Stanley stumbled upon him in the village of Ujiji and posed the famous question, "Dr. Livingstone, I presume?"

David Livingstone was headstrong, quarrelsome, and self centered, but his devotion and dedication to Africa overshadow his flaws. He remains one of the greatest explorers of the nineteenth century and the man who almost singlehandedly opened the "unknown Africa" to the outside world. This is his story.

O N E

A Son of the Mills

David Livingstone was born on March 19, 1813, in the tiny town of Blantrye, Scotland, 8 miles (13 kilometers) south of the city of Glasgow. His family was poor but respectable. His father, Neil, was a traveling tea salesman who passed out religious tracts to his customers with the zeal of a missionary. Both he and his wife, Agnes Hunter, were devout members of the Independent Congregational Church. Self-taught, Neil Livingstone knew the value of a good education and made sure that his seven children went to school.

Normal schooling, however, ended for David when he turned ten. It was replaced by long hours at the Blantrye Works cotton mill. He was not alone. Of the hundreds of mill workers in the town, three quarters of them were children. In the early days of the Industrial Revolution, child labor was commonplace. Livingstone worked fourteen hours a day at the mill with only short breaks for lunch and dinner, six days

A castle in Blantyne, Scotland—the hometown of David Livingstone. A life of wealth and ease was unknown to the Livingstones, though, who lived in relative poverty.

a week. He arrived at 6:00 a.m. and did not leave work until 8:00 p.m.

While the mill owners were demanding, they did provide night classes for their school-age workers. Attendance was voluntary, and Livingstone's parents encouraged him to go, which he did willingly. After work, he went directly to night school where he attended classes in Latin, math, science, and theology from 8:00 to 10:00 p.m. Then he returned to his family's tiny, one-room tenement apartment and read until midnight or later. He would do this, he later wrote, "if my mother did not interfere by jumping up and snatching the books out of my hands." He kept to this punishing schedule for thirteen years.

Livingstone was such a bookworm that he would often read at work as well. "My reading while at work was carried on by placing the book on a portion of the spinning-jenny [a machine] so that I could catch sentence after sentence as I passed at my work; I thus kept up a pretty constant study undisturbed by the roar of the machinery."

He later attributed his ability to read and write under any condition in the wilds of Africa to this early training.

Although his parents were devout, Livingstone did not experience a deeply religious conversion until the age of twenty. A year later, still working in the mill, he read a pamphlet about the need for medically trained Christian missionaries in Asia and Africa. He decided to devote his life to this cause and enrolled, with his family's financial help, at Anderson's University (now the University of Strathclyde) in Glasgow to study medicine. He continued to work summers at the mill to support himself. Livingstone graduated with a medical degree four years later, in 1840, and was accepted into the seminary of the London Missionary Society for his initial training.

Livingstone dreamed of going to China as a missionary. But fate intervened. In 1839 Great Britain entered into the first Opium War with China. It would be impossible for him to travel to China under these conditions. That same year, he attended a lecture given by the celebrated African missionary Robert Moffat who was home on leave. Moffat's eloquence and his total commitment to serving God in Africa inspired Livingstone. The two later became friends. "I have sometimes seen, in the morning sun, the smoke of a thousand villages, where no missionary has ever been," Moffat once told him.

Livingstone was ordained a minister in early 1840 and sent off to South Africa in December of that year. He arrived in Cape Town in March 1841, four days shy of his twenty-eighth birthday. He would not see his homeland again for sixteen years.

CHILD LABOR

Child labor was one of the greatest social problems to come out of the Industrial Revolution. The practice developed in England and Scotland in the eighteenth century. Mine and factory owners quickly discovered that children were a cheap and obedient source of unskilled labor. Parents, mired in poverty, allowed children as young as six to go to work to bring much-needed income home for the family. These children worked long hours often under hazardous conditions.

The first law regulating child labor was established in Great Britain in 1802, but it took another thirty years before there was firm enforcement of such laws. Child labor was also prevalent in Canada and the United States. By 1832 one third of America's factory workers were children. Although child labor is a thing of the past in most of the English-speaking world, children continue to make up a portion of the migrant agricultural workforce in the United States.

Child labor was a grim fact of life in nineteenth-century England. These child workers are carrying clay to be made into bricks.

T W O

A Missionary in Africa

It took the young Livingstone ten weeks to make the arduous 700-mile (1,127-kilometer) journey by oxcart north from Port Elizabeth, South Africa, to Kuruman, the mission station founded and run by his mentor Doctor Moffat. Livingstone quickly came to love the African countryside and its people. He learned their languages and studied their cultures and customs. He did not connect as strongly with many of the Europeans there, especially the Dutch settlers called Boers, farmers who were born in South Africa, which had once been a Dutch colony. Most Boers had little respect for the Africans and exploited them as laborers.

Livingstone did not get along with many of his fellow missionaries either. He even came to resent Moffat and yearned to run his own mission deeper in the interior where no other missionary had yet gone.

After spending two years at Kuruman, Livingstone was given permission from the society to head 200 miles (322 kilometers) north

Besides being a dedicated and effective missionary, Robert Moffat, Livingstone's mentor, translated the Bible and other religious works into the African language Tswana.

The English Missionary Movement

England had virtually no missionary movement until 1792, when William Carey, a shoemaker and Baptist preacher, founded the Baptist Missionary Society. According to Carey, he received the call to convert the "heathen" in foreign lands to Christianity in his cobbler's shop and cried out, "Here am I; send me!"

The following year, Carey and his family went to India to establish a mission. For seven years he converted no one and watched his wife lose her health and die. Eventually things turned around as the mission began to take hold and succeed. By the time of his death in 1834, Carey's mission was thriving and included a newly established college for converts at the town of Serampore.

Carey's example and his missionary society inspired other Christian denominations. The London Missionary Society concentrated its efforts on Africa, where it sent young Robert Moffat in 1816. His mission at Kuruman became one of the first successful ventures in South Africa. Like Carey, Moffat was a skilled linguist and translated the Bible into the African language of Tswana.

The London Missionary Society was concerned with both the physical and the spiritual well-being of the Africans and trained its missionaries in medicine as well as religion. Although missionaries were later identified with European imperialism, in the early nineteenth century they were seen as a positive force in Africa and Asia and as a counter to the racism of many European colonists.

William Carey, seen here with a Brahmin, a representative
of the highest class in Indian society, devoted his life
to missionary work in southern Asia.

to the village of Mabotsa on the Limpopo River. There, he set up a new mission with Roger Edwards. But predictably, Livingstone did not get along with Edwards, who was eighteen years his senior. He wrote letters to the director of the London Missionary Society, criticizing both Edwards and Moffat.

It was at Mabotsa that Livingstone had one of the most harrowing experiences of his life. The area was plagued by a group of lions that were killing the livestock. Livingstone felt that if he killed one of the lions, the others would leave the area. Accompanied by several African hunters, he went out to hunt down a lion. They tracked one to a small wooded area. Although they encircled the woods, the lion escaped and charged Livingstone. He shot it with his rifle, and it fell, wounded. As he was reloading his weapon, the lion lunged at him again. Livingstone later wrote ". . . he caught my shoulder as he sprang, and we both came to the ground below together. Growling horribly close to my ear, he shook me as a terrier dog does a rat."

Two hunters came to Livingstone's aid and were also mauled by the wounded beast. Together, they managed to kill it. Livingstone suffered eleven gashes, and his upper left arm was broken in three places. With amazing stamina and courage, he set the broken bone and sutured the wounds himself without anesthetic. The shattered arm was never the same, and Livingstone lost most of the use of it. He claimed that the experience, however, was beneficial, having made him unafraid of death.

To recuperate from his injuries, Livingstone returned to Kuruman where he met, and eventually fell in love with, Robert Moffat's daughter Mary. Livingstone probably sensed that she would make a good missionary wife, having spent most of her life in Africa with her father. They were married on January 2, 1845.

Livingstone took his bride back to Mabotsa, but he was not happy there. After quarreling with Edwards about the running of the mission,

Livingstone had many brushes with death during his years in Africa, but one never so close as when he was attacked by a wounded lion in 1843.

he decided to establish a mission of his own. He settled in the distant village of Kolobeng, which bordered the harsh Kalahari Desert.

The residents of Kolobeng came to respect Livingstone. He was far from the helpless missionary whose only talent was preaching. He built his own house, while Mary made her own clothes, candles, and soap. The native people confided in Livingstone about a great lake to the

Mary Livingstone was spirited, hardworking, and not prone to complain—good qualities for a missionary's wife to possess.

north that Europeans had never seen. It was called Lake Ngami, and Livingstone decided he would try to find it. His reasons for doing so were complicated. He wanted to set up a mission there among the Makololo people who inhabited the region. He also had the notion that if he could open up Africa's interior to Western civilization and trade, the horrors of the lucrative slave trade in central Africa would be crushed by more legitimate commerce. Livingstone also wanted to find the lake for the sheer thrill of discovery. Within this determined missionary doctor beat the heart of a true explorer.

The lake was 300 miles (483 kilometers) away and to get there Livingstone would have to mount a full expedition. William Colton Oswell, a wealthy big-game hunter Livingstone had befriended, shared the missionary's sense of adventure and agreed to finance the expedition. On June 1, 1849, Livingstone, Oswell, and their friend Mungo Murray set off where no European had gone before.

THREE

An Explorer Is Born

The long trek to Lake Ngami was filled with hardships and danger. It took the expedition two months to cross the Kalahari Desert, during which they ran out of water and were forced to dig for it. They also became lost numerous times.

On July 4, 1849, the group reached the Zouga River, which the local residents told them was fed by the Ngami River. They followed the Zouga north for another 280 miles (451 kilometers) and reached the northeastern corner of Lake Ngami in present-day Botswana on August 1. The Makololo people, however, to whom Livingstone hoped to minister, lived an unexpected additional 200 miles (322 kilometers) to the north. Since the local chief refused to provide the expedition with guides, Livingstone reluctantly returned to Kolobeng.

Arriving home in October, Livingstone reported his discovery of Lake Ngami to the London Missionary Society. The Royal Geographical

Livingstone, in the lead with one of his sons, arrives at Lake Ngami, his first major discovery in Africa during an earlier expedition.

Society in London received the news as well and recognized Livingstone's achievement with a gift of twenty-five guineas, equal to about $127. As would be the pattern with many other British explorers in Africa, Livingstone barely mentioned the contributions of his associates Oswell and Murray in his report.

Livingstone's first taste of exploration only whetted his appetite for more. He prepared another expedition to Ngami. This time he intended to take along his pregnant wife and their three children, despite his father-in-law's objections.

The expedition was a difficult one. Two of the Livingstone children came down with the dreaded disease of malaria. So the group stopped only briefly at Lake Ngami and then returned to Kolobeng. Shortly after, Mary gave birth to a girl, who also contracted malaria and died six weeks later.

Malaria—The Dreaded Jungle Fever

Malaria, the disease that plagued Livingstone for much of his life in Africa, is transmitted to humans by the bite of one of about sixty different kinds of mosquitoes. Malaria victims suffer recurring chills and fever, muscle pain, headaches, and nausea. In the most serious cases—known as jungle fever—the parasitic organisms that cause malaria block the brain's blood vessels, which can lead to coma and even death.

The traditional treatment for malaria is quinine, a drug extracted from the bark of the cinchona tree. In the twentieth century, two synthetic drugs, Atabrise and chloroquine, have proved to be more effective than quinine at both curing and preventing malaria.

Although the disease has been largely eradicated in Europe and the Americas since 1950, malaria remains a major illness in Africa, Southeast Asia, and the more tropical regions of South America, where about 300 million cases are reported each year. Researchers are developing malaria vaccines that may one day wipe out this dreaded disease once and for all.

Quinine, a powdered medicine made from cinchona bark, was not only used to treat malaria but fever and general pain as well.

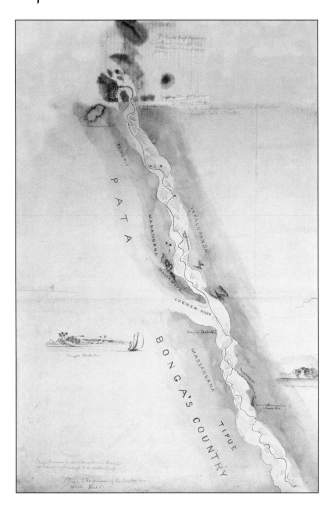

Livingstone created this hand-drawn map showing the route he took along the Zambezi River. His highly detailed maps were valuable aids to future explorers.

Livingstone, however, was determined to return north and meet with Sebituane, the chief of the Makololo. He set off once more in April 1851. Again, despite Moffat's strong objections, he took his family. Risks mounted, and this third expedition quickly proved a nightmare. Their guide deserted them, and they became hopelessly lost in the Kalahari. The children, swollen from insect bites, nearly died of thirst after four days without water. The dreaded tsetse fly attacked the livestock they had brought with them. Livingstone wrote in his journal: ". . . though we were not aware of any great number [of flies] having at any time light on our cattle, we lost 43 fine oxen by its bite."

An Explorer Is Born

On the fifth day, they reached the Mabebe River and fresh water. A few days later, they reached a tributary of the great Zambezi River, the Chobe River, which no European had ever seen.

They were then entering Makololo territory and met Chief Sebituane at his river island home. He agreed to allow Livingstone to build a mission station but died of pneumonia a short time later. Sebituane's son Sekelutu, who had replaced his father as chief, kept Sebituane's promise and helped Livingstone look for a site for his mission.

While searching, Livingstone and Oswell reached the banks of the mighty Zambezi in present-day Zambia. Livingstone was awed by this swift-running river and saw it as a possible means of traveling all the way

Livingstone put his family through many trials, by having them accompany him on two expeditions. Many questioned his judgment in deciding to bring his wife and children along.

THE ZAMBEZI RIVER

The fourth-largest river in Africa, the Zambezi winds its way from northwestern Zambia in central Africa to the Indian Ocean where it empties into the Mozambique Channel. It stretches some 1,650 miles (2,655 kilometers) and drains more than 500,000 square miles (1.3 million square kilometers) of land.

As Livingstone later learned, to his bitter disappointment, the Zambezi is not navigable for great stretches and is not a viable waterway for trade and commerce. However, in the twentieth century, Europeans and Africans have learned to use the power of its current in other ways. A hydroelectric plant was built on the river near Victoria Falls in 1938. Kariba Dam, a hydroelectric dam 200 miles (322 kilometers) downstream from the falls, was completed in 1959. It provides electrical power to Zimbabwe and Zambia and is one of the largest dams in the world.

to Africa's east coast from the interior. By following the river, Livingstone hoped, British ships could reach the interior to trade and colonize.

Oswell dismissed the idea of navigating down the Zambezi as too dangerous, but Livingstone was determined to try. He realized that before he could do so, however, he had to be sure his family was safe and settled because Mary was pregnant again. On the return trip to Kolobeng, she gave birth to their fifth child, a boy, in the desert. They named him William Oswell in honor of their colleague. Livingstone accompanied her and the children to Cape Town, where on April 23, 1852, his family embarked on a ship sailing for England.

In Cape Town, Livingstone spent three months preparing for a new expedition back to the Zambezi. "I will open a way to the interior or perish," he wrote in a letter to his brother-in-law J. S. Moffat. Livingstone had heeded the call of adventure and would push forward, regardless of the dangers that might lie ahead.

FOUR

Crossing a Continent

On his way back to Kolobeng from Cape Town, Livingstone got news that the Boers, who hated him for defending and advocating for the African natives, were plotting to destroy his home there and all of his possessions.

Instead, they attacked and razed the nearby town of Sechele. Livingstone was forced to wait out the chaos in Kuruman and did not reach Linyanti, the capital city of the Makololo, until May 23, 1853. He remained there for nearly six months, sick with malaria. When he was well enough to travel, he and twenty-seven porters followed the Zambezi River north into the Portuguese colony of Angola. His goal was to reach the Atlantic coast at the port of Luanda, a journey no one had made successfully. Along the way he was confronted with hostile tribes, flooding, and a terrible dampness that rotted through his tents, forcing the fever-sick missionary to sleep on the wet ground. At one point,

The Boers, Dutch settlers in South Africa, were an obstacle to Livingstone's missionary work among the region's native peoples. The group captured in this photograph was prepared to defend their homes from the British during the Boer War of 1900.

his bearers threatened to mutiny, and he faced them down with a loaded pistol and remarkable courage.

He reached Luanda on May 31, 1854. Weak and deathly ill, Livingstone could have easily accepted the British consul's offer of a passage home to England, but he refused to do so. He felt it was his responsibility to see that the loyal Africans who had accompanied him on his 1,500-mile (2,414-kilometer) journey were returned safely to their homes. He did agree to send his maps and personal journals on a British ship. The ship later sank in the Atlantic, and the record of his journey was lost.

Slowly, but determinedly, Livingstone made his way back to Linyanti. Along the way he was again beset by difficulties. A tree branch

Stricken with malaria and other illnesses, often too weak to walk,
Livingstone was carried by his porters on a litter.

snapped back into his face, temporarily injuring his eyes and nearly blinding him. He contracted rheumatic fever, which almost claimed his hearing. When he at last reached Linyanti, he rested for seven weeks before resuming travel. Having made it to the western coast of Africa, Livingstone was resolved to reach the eastern coast from the interior. He hoped to get there by following the Zambezi River to its mouth. He set off on November 3, 1855, with a party of porters and guides provided by Chief Sekelutu.

Livingstone expected the river to lose elevation as it flowed to the Indian Ocean, but that was not the case. The mile-wide river seemed to go on forever. One day Livingstone heard a roaring sound like thunder in the distance. The guides grew excited and spoke of "Mosi-oa-tunya," which means "the smoke that thunders."

As they drew nearer, Livingstone saw the smoke, which was actually mist, and then farther ahead of their boat a break in the earth in which the raging water rushed down into darkness. "From this cloud rushed up a great jet of vapor exactly like steam," he wrote in his journal, "and it mounted two hundred or three hundred feet [61 to 91 meters] high; there, condensing, it changed its hue to that of dark smoke, and came back in a constant shower, which soon wetted us to the skin."

But Livingstone was so excited by this great discovery, he hardly noticed the dousing. He managed to paddle a canoe out to an island that breached the edge of the magnificent falls. He dropped a weighted rope over the edge to measure the depth of the chasm. It measured more than 340 feet (104 meters).

Livingstone decided to name the falls in honor of England's queen. He later called Victoria Falls "the most wonderful sight I have seen in Africa."

Livingstone continued down the Zambezi, crossing the Kaloma River on November 30. Days and weeks passed quickly as the explorer

This lush landscape near Victoria Falls was painted by England's Thomas Baines, who was an explorer in addition to an artist. Note the herd of buffalo shrouded in mist on the cliff.

made his way along the swift-running river. In the last stretch, impatient to arrive at the coast, Livingstone abandoned the river and headed off on foot for the last 50 miles (80 kilometers). He thus completely missed a

VICTORIA FALLS

While not the tallest waterfall in the world, Victoria Falls remains one of the most spectacular. The 343-foot (105-meter) plunge of the mighty Zambezi River into a deep and narrow chasm has lost none of its breathtaking beauty since Livingstone first laid eyes on it.

A railroad bridge was built across the gorge below the falls in 1905. The bridge offers passengers an up-close view of the falls. The British colonial authority in Zimbabwe granted protected status to this natural wonder in 1931, and it was designated a national park in 1952. Visitors from around the world come to the 8-square-mile (21-square-kilometer) park to view the falls' marvels and see the wide array of plant and animal life that inhabit the area, including blood lilies, baboons, and crocodiles.

section of the river that descended into the Kebrabasa Gorge, an almost unnavigable stretch. This lack of familiarity with a critical portion of the Zambezi would come to haunt him later.

Weak, exhausted, but triumphant, Livingstone arrived at the port city of Quelimone in what is now Mozambique on May 20, 1856. In three years he had traveled 4,300 miles (6,920 kilometers). He had crossed the continent of Africa from west to east, a feat no European

Victoria Falls, first discovered by Livingstone in 1855, is today one of the most popular tourist destinations in Africa.

before him had accomplished. He had also been the first European to lay eyes on the spectacle of Victoria Falls and the other wonders that awaited him along the way. At last, he was ready to return to Great Britain. He had left his homeland sixteen years earlier an unknown missionary doctor. He would return a national hero.

FIVE

A Triumphant Homecoming

David Livingstone arrived in England aboard a royal naval vessel in December 1856. News of his extraordinary achievements in Africa preceded him. Crowds of admirers mobbed him wherever he went. He was sought after by journalists for interviews and by colleges and organizations for lectures. At first this attention was cause for anxiety for the retiring missionary, who had spoken little English in his sixteen years in Africa. He quickly proved, however, a popular and inspiring speaker. A speech he delivered at Cambridge University so moved students and teachers that they founded the Universities Missions for Christian Work in Africa.

Livingstone was showered with honors. Cambridge, Oxford, and Glasgow universities gave him honorary degrees. The Royal Geographical Society made him a fellow and gave him its highest award, a gold medal. The society's president, Sir Roderick Murchison, called

THE ROYAL GEOGRAPHICAL SOCIETY

The Royal Society, as it is called, has played a major role in world exploration since it was founded in England in 1830. Through financial aid and its official support, the society has helped promote the careers of many explorers, including David Livingstone.

While research and exploration are still important to the society today, it is also heavily involved in the areas of conservation, preservation, and education. The Expedition Advisory Center conducts seminars and workshops at various universities for student researchers and their projects in the field. Included in the nearly 12,000 current members of the Royal Society are professional geographers and professors as well as many laypeople with a keen interest in geography and exploration. Many members make use of the society's London headquarters, which features a voluminous library and a map room containing close to a million maps, charts, atlases, and written records.

Livingstone's journey across Africa "the greatest triumph in geographical research . . . in our times." The explorer was even granted a private audience with Queen Victoria, whose name he had made a permanent part of African geography.

Livingstone was persuaded to write a book based on his journals.

In this editorial cartoon, Livingstone is shown unlocking central Africa. The illustration reflects the high regard the Western world held for him after he returned from his initial successes in 1856.

Entitled *Missionary Travels and Researches in South Africa* and published in 1857, it sold 12,000 copies before it was even released and became a runaway best-seller. The effort, however, was a torturous one, and the author swore he would rather cross Africa again than write another book. The book's royalties gave his family the financial security they had never known and helped finance his next expedition to Africa.

Livingstone was completely committed to exploration, and when the London Missionary Society expressed concern about his exploring taking precedence over his missionary work, he readily resigned his position. In truth, Livingstone had found a new cause. His goal was to spread European values and civilization to Africa and to promote, through his explorations, new means of access to the interior. By doing so, he still believed legitimate commerce would replace and put an end, once and

THE AFRICAN SLAVE TRADE

Slavery had existed in Africa for centuries, but it grew to enormous proportions in the seventeenth century when Europeans first established colonies in the West Indies. The English, Dutch, and French colonists sought out African slaves to work their large cotton, tobacco, and coffee plantations in the New World.

African peoples captured men, women, and children of other tribes and sold them to Arab slave traders. The traders took the slaves in one of two directions. To the east were the slave markets on the island of Zanzibar. Slaves were generally sold there and then shipped to India. The western coast was also known as the Slave Coast. There, slaves were sold to Europeans who loaded them onto ships and took them across the Atlantic to the West Indies, the American South, or Brazil. At least one out of five slaves died during this terrible leg of the journey, known as the Middle Passage, which could take as much as ten weeks.

The British Parliament passed an antislavery bill in 1807, but slave trading continued in the Dutch colonies in Africa and in parts of South America. Largely through Livingstone's efforts, the practice came under increasing attack from the British government and eventually was ended. While slavery no longer exists in most parts of the English-speaking world today, it persists in the Sudan in Africa and in parts of South America and Asia.

This slave convoy was an all too common sight in
central Africa in the 1850s and 1860s.

Charles Livingstone, who accompanied his older brother to Africa in 1858, co-wrote David's second book, The Zambezi and Its Tributaries.

for all, to the terrible slave trade, which he called "that enormous evil."

The British government appointed Livingstone consul for the east coast of Africa and commissioned him to continue his explorations of the Zambezi River and its tributaries. He was given a steamship that he christened the *Ma-Robert*, the name the native people affectionately called Mary Livingstone. She would accompany her husband on this new expedition, along with their son Oswell and a group of six scientists and artists. Among this group was Livingstone's brother Charles and botanist John Kirk.

On February 13, 1858, a "Farewell Livingstone Festival" was held in the great man's honor, attended by 350 of the most prominent people in England. Not everyone approved of such tributes, though. Among Livingstone's detractors was Lord Clarendon, head of the Foreign Office. In a letter to Sir Roderick Murchison, who organized the festival, Lord Clarendon wrote, "For some past, I thought Dr. L. was being too much honored for his own good, and that the public was being led to expect more from his future labors than will probably be realized."

Lord Clarendon's words would prove sadly prophetic.

S I X

Fallen Hero

David Livingstone returned to Africa with the highest of expectations. But almost from the beginning, his second tour of Africa was a disaster. Mary took ill on the ocean crossing and remained in Cape Town to recuperate while the rest of the party headed north to the Zambezi. Livingstone would not see her again for nearly four years.

The party chugged up the Zambezi in the *Ma-Robert*, winding to its mouth. The last stretch of the river, which Livingstone foolishly had not scouted previously, proved unnavigable by the *Ma-Robert*. It was filled with shallow spots, sandbars, and the treacherous Kebrabasa Rapids, where the party almost drowned trying to pass through. In every way, the *Ma-Robert* was to prove the wrong vessel for African waterways, eating up precious fuel and breaking down frequently.

Sickness and the rigors of Africa continued to dog the expedition. One man died of malaria after losing his supply of quinine in the river.

The Ma-Robert is shown running into trouble in the shallow waters of the lower Zambezi River. Livingstone's failure to anticipate this potential problem spelled disaster for his expedition.

To make matters worse, Livingstone was at constant odds with his companions. Those who questioned his decisions, such as naval officer Commodore Bedingfield, soon left the expedition. But the person who most drew Livingstone's wrath was his own brother. Charles Livingstone was the most insufferable and selfish member of the expedition.

After being faced with another impassable stretch, this time on the Shire River, a tributary of the Zambezi, Livingstone temporarily abandoned his steamship and went overland to Lake Nyasa, a long narrow waterway to the north. Today it is called Lake Malawi. Through the summer of 1859 he made several futile attempts to reach the lake via the Shire and finally gave up in frustration.

Livingstone returned overland to Lake Nyasa and was met there by the Universities Mission to the Shire Highlands, which he had helped to establish in England. He had high hopes that the group, led by Bishop Mackenzie, would found a permanent mission station in the region. But within a year Mackenzie and several others died of fever, the mission was abandoned, and Livingstone's dreams were left unfulfilled.

Mary, who had returned to England from Cape Town, sought consolation from her loneliness in alcohol. She returned to Africa in January 1862, but her reunion with her husband in Kangone was brief. She contracted a powerful strain of malaria and died in excruciating pain in April. Livingstone was devastated by her death. "It feels as if heart and strength were taken out of me—my horizon is all dark," he wrote to a friend.

After four years, Livingstone had little to show for his second expedition in Africa. In 1863 the British government, disappointed in his failure to find a navigable waterway across the interior, recalled him. He was in no rush to get home. Fearing that African slavers would claim and use his new ship, the *Lady Nyasa*, he piloted it from the east coast of Africa across the Indian Ocean to Bombay (now called Mumbai), India. There he sold it and booked passage to England. He arrived on July 23, 1864.

Livingstone did not receive the enthusiastic hero's welcome of his first homecoming. The newspapers had found a new hero to fawn over—explorer John Hanning Speke. Speke, who had explored Africa with the adventurer Richard Francis Burton, had discovered Lake

JOHN HANNING SPEKE

One of Livingstone's chief rivals in Africa, John Hanning Speke came to the exploring trade from a very different background. He was the son of a wealthy English family and joined the British Army at age seventeen. Speke was sent to India where he served for ten years before deciding to explore Africa. On the way there, he met Richard Francis Burton, who joined him in an ill-fated expedition to Somalia. After serving in the Crimean War, Speke again teamed up with Burton to explore central Africa. In February 1858 the two men discovered Lake Tanganyika. Later that same year, Speke, leaving an ill Burton behind, was the first European to gaze on Lake Victoria, which he believed was the main source of the Nile River, the longest waterway on the continent. Burton, who later broke off his friendship with Speke, argued that he was wrong.

A public debate between the two explorers was arranged in September 1864. The day before the debate, Speke accidentally shot himself while hunting and died.

John Hanning Speke was one of Livingstone's rivals in African exploration until his early death in 1864.

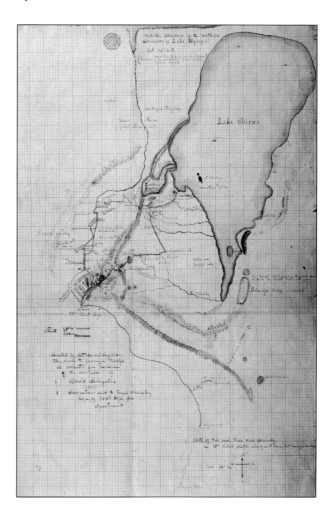

The Shire River (a tributary of the Zambezi) and Lake Shirwa are shown along with Livingstone's route on this map the explorer made himself.

Victoria in 1858 in east-central Africa. Still, Livingstone remained a popular figure with the public, if not the government and the press.

The search for the source of the Nile was one that interested every African explorer. If a water route from central to northern Africa could be found, it would provide the means for commerce and trade that Europeans dreamed of. Livingstone had his own ideas about the Nile's source. He believed the Bangweolo River and its associated lake of the same name, two bodies of water he had explored, were part of a series of linking waterways that eventually fed into both the Nile and the Congo rivers. He expounded this theory in his second book, *The Zambesi and Its Tributaries*, published in 1865. Based on the strength of Livingstone's argument, the Royal Geographical Society gave him the opportunity to return to Africa to further explore the Bangweolo River and other waterways that might be the source of the two major rivers. The Foreign Office agreed to make Livingstone British consul for the region stretching between Portuguese East Africa and Ethiopia. This time, however, they gave him only 500 pounds ($2,500) to prepare his expedition. The Royal Society matched this amount, but Livingstone had to rely on the generosity of a friend, James Young, to meet the expenses not covered by the societies' stipends.

He left England in August 1865. This time he took no colleagues with him. Whatever adventures and challenges awaited him in Africa, he would face them alone.

SEVEN

Lost in Africa

Livingstone's last journey to Africa started on the island of Zanzibar where he arrived on March 9, 1866. He spent the next seven weeks hiring assistants and porters for his expedition into the interior. Among the Africans he engaged were two men who would remain his loyal followers to the end—James Chuma and David Susi.

With a passport signed by the sultan of Zanzibar, Livingstone, Chuma, Susi, and sixty porters followed the coastline south to the mouth of the Ruvuma River. They then followed the river northward eventually turning south to Lake Nyasa. From there they headed northwest to reach the southern tip of Lake Tanganyika. By this time, the expedition was in a desperate state. Disease and illness again dogged their every step. Livingstone contracted rheumatic fever, which he could not treat because one of the porters had run off with his precious medicine chest.

One of Zanzibar's longest-serving sultans, Barghash helped Livingstone return to mainland Africa in 1866 by signing his passport.

"I feel as if I had now received sentence of death," he wrote in his journal. Another careless porter broke the chronometer, a timing instrument that determined longitude at sea, and the explorer soon lost his bearings. Too weak to go on, he found help from a most unlikely source—a party of Arab slave traders. They treated him with care and kindness and accompanied him to Lake Mweru to the west of Tanganyika. From there Livingstone explored the Luapula River and Lake Bangweolo to the south, thinking they were part of the linking waterways that he believed formed the source of the Nile.

As Livingstone traveled farther and farther into the heart of Africa, he lost all touch with the outside world. Rumors began to circulate, probably spread by slavers and disgruntled porters from his expedition, that he had been killed by members of his own party. One such report reached the British governor of Zanzibar, and he conveyed the news to the West. Several newspapers even published obituaries of Livingstone. However, in early 1867, the Royal Geographical Society received letters from Livingstone proving that he was still very much alive. But no one seemed to know where he was. No word of the great explorer's whereabouts had been received throughout 1868 and into 1869.

James Gordon Bennett, the colorful publisher of the New York *Herald Tribune*, sensed a great story in the Livingstone mystery. He decided to send one of his reporters to Africa to search for the great man. The correspondent he picked for the job was a former Civil War soldier who had spent the last few years drifting and writing. Henry Morton Stanley had the two qualifications that Bennett sought: He had a sense of

Looking every inch the fearless explorer, newspaperman Henry Morton Stanley got the scoop of the century when he "found" David Livingstone alive and well in Africa.

LIVINGSTONE'S LAST HOME

It is ironic that Livingstone's home base in his last years in Africa served as a center for the slave and ivory trade, two practices that he condemned.

The first Europeans to pass through Ujiji were Richard Francis Burton and John Hanning Speke, in 1858 while on their way to Lake Tanganyika. Following Livingstone's death, the town remained in Arab control until 1891, when German colonists took it over as part of German East Africa.

Today Ujiji is a suburb of Kigoma City in west Tanzania and is the region's oldest community. No longer known for the slave trade, today it is probably best known for its fisheries.

adventure, and he was a talented writer. Bennett was prepared to give Stanley all the funds he needed to mount a major expedition into Africa, but he had to, as he wrote him, "FIND LIVINGSTONE."

Meanwhile, Livingstone, battling ill health, was nearly alone. All that remained of his party were Chuma, Susi, and two other faithful Africans. They traveled overland with an Arab trader to the town of

Ujiji, just east of Lake Tanganyika. Weak and nearly delirious with fever, Livingstone almost did not make it. "Pneumonia of right lung, and I cough all day and all night," he wrote in his journal on January 7, 1869. ". . . If I look at any piece of wood, the back seems covered over with the figures and faces of men, and they remain, though I look away . . ."

On his arrival at Ujiji in March 1869, Livingstone was shocked to find that the supplies sent ahead for him had been stolen. Despite this setback, he made Ujiji his home base. Too sick to travel far, he spent much of the next year writing in his journal and reading his Bible.

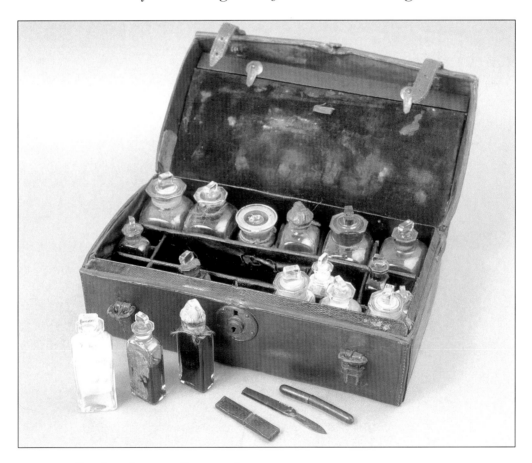

This leather medicine chest was Livingstone's protection against disease and death. Prized and necessary possessions, his medical supplies were frequently stolen, though.

Livingstone's last years in Africa were marred by illness, frustration, and loneliness.

Completely alone except for his few faithful African assistants, Livingstone refused to give up his search for the source of the Nile. It was the one passion that continued to drive him. In March 1871, he set out one more time for the Lualaba River near the village of Nyangwe. It was Livingstone's stubborn belief that the Lualaba was the crucial link to the Nile, when in fact, it was the source of the Congo River, farther to the west.

While resting at Nyangwe, another slave-trading post, Livingstone witnessed a terrible event. A group of Arab slave traders opened fire in the marketplace, killing a number of native women, children, and elderly people. His followers had to restrain Livingstone from going to the aid of the massacred. Afterward, Livingstone was anxious to get as far away from the slavers and their violence as possible. With Chuma, Susi, and a few others, he made the 350-mile (563-kilometer) journey on foot back to Ujiji, which he had not seen for more than two years. It was a difficult and painful trek for the ill explorer, and when he arrived there on October 23, 1871, he discovered once more that his goods and medicine had been stolen, this time by an Arab sheriff.

Livingstone had reached the lowest point of his career as an explorer. He was sick and without supplies and medicine in a lonely outpost far from civilization. He was completely helpless. What he did not know was that help was on the way.

E I G H T

"Dr. Livingstone, I Presume?"

By fall 1871, Henry Morton Stanley, intrepid journalist, was steadily making his way toward Ujiji. Yet he had initially been reluctant to take up Bennett's challenge. Like many people, he believed that Livingstone was most likely dead. If he was alive, finding him in the unknown reaches of the interior of Africa was a daunting proposition even for a seasoned adventurer like Stanley. The reporter's search for Livingstone got off to a slow start. He first traveled to Egypt, where he witnessed the opening of the Suez Canal on November 16, 1869. From Egypt, he traveled through the Middle East, stopping in Jerusalem; Constantinople, Turkey; and Teheran, Iran. He finally reached Bombay, India, where Livingstone had been several times, and then sailed for Zanzibar, where he arrived in January 1871. With an extensive expedition, Stanley made his way inland to the trading center of Tabora in present-day Tanzania, where he set up his home base. Eighty miles (129 kilometers) from

"Dr. Livingstone, I Presume?"

Henry Morton Stanley (right) consults a map with his fellow explorers. His meeting with David Livingstone inspired Stanley to explore Africa himself.

Ujiji, Stanley met the Arab caravan that had brought Livingstone back to that town. Overcome with excitement at the news, Stanley pushed on. He arrived in Ujiji on November 10, 1871, although the exact date has been questioned.

Only a mile from the town, Stanley, dressed in his best safari uniform, ordered his men to display the American flag, fire their guns, and sound their horns. Thousands of townspeople, including Chuma and Susi, gathered to see them march into Ujiji. Livingstone's loyal companions met Stanley and then rushed off to tell Livingstone the news. Livingstone waited in front of his modest hut for the white man who Susi had mistakenly called "an Englishman." As an excited crowd gathered around the approaching expedition, Stanley slowly proceeded through the mass of people. When he met Livingstone, he described the historic meeting in his dispatch to the *Herald Tribune*:

> There is a group of the most respectable Arabs, and as I came nearer I see the white face of an old man among them. He has a cap with a gold band around it, his dress is a short jacket of red blanket cloth and pants. I am shaking hands with him. We raise our hats, and I say:—"Dr. Livingstone, I presume?" And he says, "Yes."

Stanley probably used this oddly indirect form of address because he feared Livingstone did not like journalists and might not be pleased to see him. Nothing could have been further from the truth. Livingstone was overjoyed to see the first white man he had laid eyes on in six years. He was eager to hear what news Stanley brought from the outside world and was even more eager to get the supplies, mail, and medicine the reporter had brought with him. The younger man's respect and genuine interest were just the tonic Livingstone needed to revive his spirits. "You have brought me new life," he kept repeating as they talked and shared a meal in Livingstone's hut. Stanley persuaded the explorer to write a series of articles about the slave trade for the *Herald Tribune*

This depiction of the historic meeting of Henry Morton Stanley and David Livingstone in Ujiji was based on Livingstone's memory of the event.

that proved influential in raising public protest in England against it.

As for Stanley, he fell under the older man's spell and eventually became an African explorer himself. "I was converted by him," Stanley later wrote, "although he tried not to do it."

Stanley accompanied Livingstone on a short expedition to the northern end of Lake Tanganyika to find a river they believed would connect the body of water to Lake Victoria. They found the river, but it flowed into, not out of, Lake Tanganyika. Again, Livingstone had failed to find a link to the Nile. The pair returned to Ujiji and then set out for

Henry Morton Stanley

    Henry Stanley's meeting with David Livingstone was one of the defining moments of his life. Inspired by the older man, Stanley went on to become one of the most successful African explorers of his day.

    Adventure, however, was nothing new to the American journalist. Born John Rowlands in Wales, a part of Great Britain, he went to sea at age seventeen as a cabin boy. Arriving in New Orleans, Louisiana, in 1858, he took the name of Henry Morton Stanley, a cotton merchant he worked for.

    During the Civil War, young Stanley served in the Confederate army for a time and then the Union navy. After the war, he became a newspaper correspondent covering events and wars in such far-flung places as Crete, Spain, and Ethiopia.

    In 1874, a year after Livingstone's death, Stanley returned to Africa to continue the great explorer's work. Over the next fifteen years he explored much of central Africa. He circumnavigated Lake Victoria, surveyed Lake Tanganyika, and attempted to trace the sources of the Nile. He also traveled the length of the Congo River and helped open the region for the Belgians. Ironically, Livingstone's successor unknowingly helped establish one of the most notorious and repressive slave-trading colonies on the continent—the misnamed Congo Free State, later to become the Belgian Congo.

After returning to England, Stanley was knighted by the government for his achievements as an explorer and served as a member of Parliament from 1895 to 1900. He died in 1904, nearly as famous in death as his great friend, David Livingstone.

Henry Morton Stanley and David Livingstone journey on the Rusizi
River as part of their only joint expedition.

Tabora, Stanley's home base. It was there, four months after their first meeting, that Stanley and Livingstone parted. Stanley tried to persuade the explorer to return to England with him, but Livingstone insisted he could not go home without finding the Nile's source.

Before leaving for the coast, Stanley promised to send Livingstone new supplies and porters from Zanzibar. As they said their farewells, Livingstone, the tough old explorer, had to turn away, for there were tears in his eyes. Once again, he was alone in Africa.

NINE

Last Journey

Livingstone was in no condition to embark on yet another expedition in search of the Nile's source. Yet on August 25, 1872, he set out with fifty-seven porters and the ever-faithful Chuma and Susi and headed south beyond Lake Tanganyika. From there the expedition crossed the Kalangosi River bound for Lake Bangweolo.

Once again, the conditions were terrible. January 1873 saw the worst rainy season in memory. The party had to contend with heavy rains, mud, and blood-sucking leeches. Many porters contracted malaria and other diseases. In previous years, Livingstone would have been able to bear these difficulties with stolid indifference, but he was in failing health. His spirit, however, remained as strong and determined as ever, even as his body was slowly giving out. He continued to write his daily observations in small pocket books. When they were all filled, he wrote on yellowed newspaper sewn together.

On February 13, 1873, the party sighted Lake Bangweolo. It was only 80 miles (129 kilometers) away, but with the rain and the mud, it took them two months to reach it. On the last day of March, sick with dysentery, Livingstone wrote, "Nothing earthly will make me give up my work in despair. I encourage myself in the Lord my God, and go forward."

Near death from disease and exhaustion, Livingstone continues along the course of what would prove to be his final expedition.

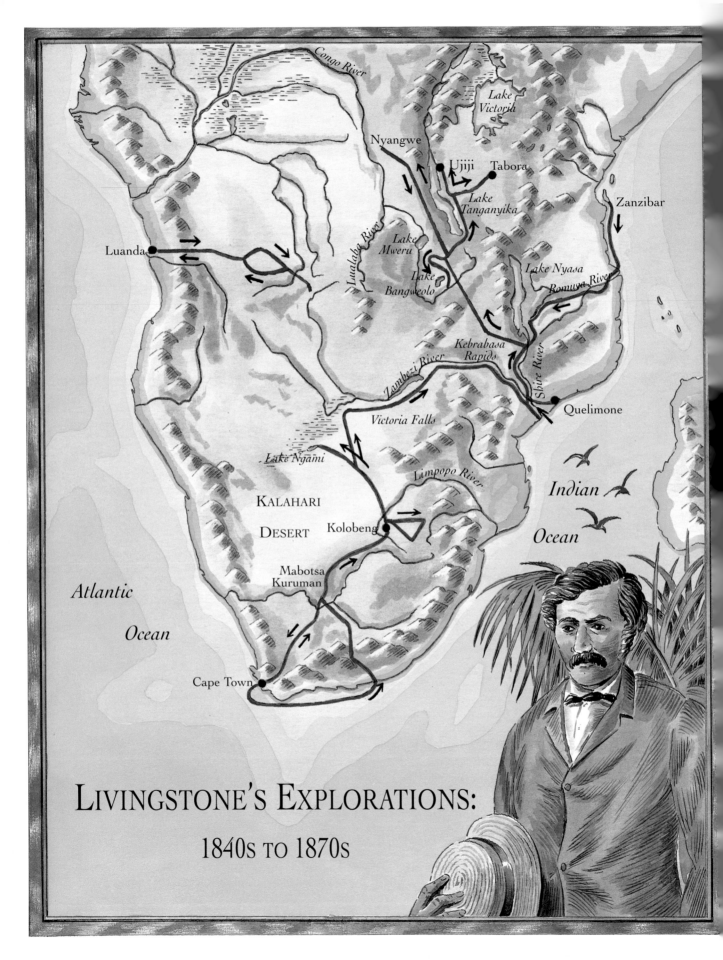

LIVINGSTONE'S EXPLORATIONS:

1840s TO 1870s

Go forward he did, doggedly dragging his battered, failing body. "It is not all pleasure, this exploration," he wrote in terse understatement on April 19. "No observation now, owing to great weakness: I can scarcely hold a pencil and my [walking] stick is a burden. Tent gone; the men built a good hut for me and the luggage . . ."

Within a few days, Livingstone's legs gave out. Chuma and Susi fashioned a stretcher to carry him. The journey continued, but now it resembled a death march. They crossed the Chambeshi River and on April 29 arrived at the village of Chief Chitambo in present-day Zambia. Livingstone could go no farther. His faithful followers built another hut for him and made him as comfortable as possible. No longer able to write or even talk without effort, the great explorer was dying.

The next day, Chief Chitambo came to visit Livingstone, but Livingstone was too weak to talk and asked him to come back the following day. At four in the morning, Susi was awakened by the boy who attended to Livingstone. He said he found the old man kneeling by his bed in prayer. Surprised, Susi rushed to the hut. Livingstone, on his knees and with his head buried in his pillow, indeed appeared to be praying. But on closer examination, Susi realized that the great explorer was dead and had been so for some time.

Chuma and Susi decided that Livingstone could not be buried and forgotten in Africa but had to be taken home to his own people. Following African custom, a native man removed Livingstone's heart and put it in the same watertight tin box in which the explorer had kept his journals. They buried the box under a nearby tree. Then they rubbed salt over his body to preserve it and let it dry for two weeks. They then wrapped the preserved corpse in cloth and put it in a sack. For nearly nine months they traveled overland with the corpse, a distance of more than 1,000 miles (1,609 kilometers). They arrived on the eastern coast in February 1874. A British warship then carried Livingstone's remains to Zanzibar and from there to England. For their extraordinary effort,

Livingstone's ever-faithful companions Chuma and Susi look on as the explorer's son and a colleague pore over the explorer's papers and maps. The woman to the left is Agnes, Livingstone's daughter.

Chuma and Susi were barely thanked by the British authorities. They were, however, later honored in England with medals from the Royal Geographical Society.

Authorities in England were uncertain at first if the dried remains were indeed those of David Livingstone until someone confirmed his identity from the shriveled left shoulder, his old wound from the lion attack. April 18, the day of his funeral, was declared a day of national mourning. The funeral was one of the grandest in London's long history. Henry Morton Stanley was among the pallbearers bringing Livingstone's body to its grave site in Westminster Abbey, the resting place of many of England's most famous men and women. Part of the inscription on his tombstone reads: "Brought by faithful hands over land and sea, here rests David Livingstone, Missionary, Traveller, Philanthropist. . . . For 30 years his life was spent in an unwearied effort to evangelize the native races, to abolish the desolating slave trade of central Africa . . ."

Afterword

No explorer is as closely identified with Africa as David Livingstone. He may have opened as much as 1 million square miles (2.6 million square kilometers) of previously unexplored parts of central Africa in his three decades as an explorer. He was the first European to see the Zambezi River, Victoria Falls, and other impressive African landmarks. Livingstone showed the world that central Africa was not the desertlike wasteland many thought it to be. He singlehandedly heightened Europe's interest in Africa, which led directly to the scramble to colonize the continent that began a decade after his death.

For all of his achievements as an explorer, though, Livingstone made some grave mistakes. He fully misjudged the navigability of the Zambezi, causing his second expedition to be an almost complete disaster. His belief that a series of lakes and rivers in central Africa was the source of the Nile was later proved to be wrong. But so were the

Livingstone reads the Bible to two potential converts. His record as a missionary was not good. His only African convert to Christianity returned to his original religion within six months.

These Tanzanian children stand before an Anglican church that Livingstone had once entered. Memorials like this one show the esteem and respect still afforded Livingstone on the continent he tirelessly explored.

theories of Speke, Burton, Stanley, and other explorers regarding the source of the Nile. Not until the 1970s did photographs taken from satellites in space show that the Nile's true source is in the mountains of Burundi, between Lake Tanganyika and Lake Victoria. Nevertheless, Livingstone's tireless explorations of these and other waterways added immeasurably to the world's knowledge of central Africa and speeded its further exploration.

Although his missionary work was limited, Livingstone was a firm friend of the African people he met and lived among and took a strong stand against the slave trade when much of the world ignored or advocated it. His speeches and writings condemning slavery helped increase public awareness in England and elsewhere. The very day Livingstone died, efforts to end the slave trade were under way as British naval patrols were sent out to prevent slave ships from leaving Africa's eastern ports. In 1876 the sultan of Zanzibar forbade the transportation of slaves by land or by sea, effectively ending the African slave trade.

Although Livingstone's relations with other whites in Africa were often strained, his devotion to Africa and its often victimized people was unwavering. His empathy and understanding for the native peoples and their way of life inspired and influenced future missionaries and others who followed in his footsteps. Unlike Stanley and other African explorers, Livingstone did not seek wealth from his explorations and died a poor man.

The respect and love Livingstone felt for Africa has been returned. Throughout the continent today streets, buildings, and towns bear his name. Dozens of statues of him are found across the continent. The most moving monument to him remains the simple granite stone erected by English missionaries some fifty years after his death by the tree where Chuma and Susi buried the explorer's heart.

A man of great character and faith, Livingstone once described himself in these words: "Nowhere have I ever appeared as anything else but a servant of God, who has simply followed the leadings of His hand . . ."

DAVID LIVINGSTONE AND HIS TIMES

1813   David Livingstone is born in Blantrye, Scotland, on March 19.

1823   At age ten, he begins working in a cotton mill.

1836   He enrolls in Anderson's University in Glasgow to study medicine.

1840   Livingstone is ordained a minister and leaves for South Africa to do missionary work.

1841–43   He works at the mission station in Kuruman, South Africa.

1843   He suffers serious wounds from a lion attack at Mabotsa.

1845   He marries Mary Moffat, daughter of missionary Robert Moffat, on January 2.

1849   He begins his first expedition to Lake Ngami in central Africa.

1854–56   Livingstone becomes the first European to cross the African continent from west to east.

1856   He returns to England and is hailed a national hero.

1858–63   On his second expedition, Livingstone searches for a navigable river from central Africa to the coast.

1864   Livingstone returns to England.

1865–72   He returns to Africa to find the source of the Nile River and eventually loses touch with civilization.

1871   Journalist Henry Morton Stanley finds Livingstone at Ujiji on Lake Tanganyika on November 10.

1872   Livingstone dies on his last expedition in the village of Chief Chitambo on May 1.

1873   He is buried in Westminster Abbey on April 18.

Further Research

Books

Benge, Janet and Geoff. *David Livingstone: Africa's Trailblazer.* Seattle: YWAM Publishing, 1999.

Buxton, Meriel. *David Livingstone.* New York: Palgrave Macmillan, 2001.

Clinton, Susan. *Henry Stanley and David Livingstone.* Chicago: Children's Press, 1990.

Dugard, Martin. *Into Africa: The Epic Adventures of Stanley & Livingstone.* New York: Doubleday, 2003.

Livingstone, David. *The Life and African Explorations of Dr. David Livingstone.* New York: Cooper Square Press, 2002.

——— . *Missionary Travels in South Africa.* Santa Barbara, CA: The Narrative Press, 2001.

Stanley, Henry M. *How I Found Livingstone in Central Africa.* Mineola, NY: Dover Publications, 2001.

Worth, Richard. *Stanley and Livingstone and the Exploration of Africa in World History.* Berkeley Heights, NJ: Enslow Publishers, 2000.

Videos

Biography: Stanley and Livingstone. A & E Home Video, VHS, 2000.

Stanley and Livingstone (1939). CBS Fox Video, VHS, 1990.

Further Research

Web Sites

David Livingstone

http://www.tartans.com/articles/famscots/livingstone.html

http://www.biggar-net.co.uk/livingstone/history.html

Other African Explorers

http://africanhistory.about.com/library/weekly/aa062501a.htm

BIBLIOGRAPHY

Alter, Judy. *Extraordinary Explorers and Adventurers.* Danbury, CT: Children's Press, 2001.

Arnold, Richard. *The True Story of David Livingstone.* Chicago: Children's Press, 1964.

Baker, Daniel B., ed. *Explorers and Discovers of the World.* Detroit: Gale Research, 1993.

Headley, Joel Tyler. *Stanley and Livingstone in Africa.* Reading, PA: The Spencer Press, 1937.

Lomask, Milton. *Exploration.* New York: Scribner, 1988.

Wellman, Sam. *David Livingstone: Missionary and Explorer.* Uhrichsville, OH: Barbour Publishing, 1995.

Source Notes

Chapter 1:

p. 8: "if my mother did not interfere . . ." David Livingstone, *The Life and African Explorations of Dr. David Livingstone* (Cooper Square Press, 2002), p. 30.

p. 9: "My reading while at work . . ." Livingstone, pp. 35–36.

p. 9: "I have sometimes seen . . ." Famous Scots Web site. URL: http://www.tartans.com/articles/famscots/livingstone.html.

Chapter 2:

p. 14: "Here am I; send me!" Martin E. Marty, "The Missionary Movement," *American Heritage*, March 1978, p. 70.

p. 16: ". . . he caught my shoulder . . ." Livingstone, p. 49.

Chapter 3:

p. 22: ". . . though we were not aware . . ." Livingstone, p. 84.

p. 25: "I will open a way . . . " Richard Arnold, *The True Story of David Livingstone*, (Children's Press, 1964), p. 55.

Chapter 4:

p. 29: "From this cloud rushed up . . ." Livingstone, p. 119.

p. 29: "the most wonderful sight . . ." Martin Dugard, *Into Africa: The Epic Adventures of Stanley and Livingstone* (Doubleday, 2003), p. 99.

Chapter 5:

p. 34: "the greatest triumph . . ." Daniel B. Baker, ed. *Explorers and Discovers of the World* (Gale Research, 1993), p. 359.

p. 38: "For some past, I thought . . ." Dugard, p. 99.

Source Notes

Chapter 6:

p. 41: "It feels as if . . ." Dugard, p. 102.

Chapter 7:

p. 46: "I feel as if I had . . . " Arnold, p. 109.

p. 48: "FIND LIVINGSTONE." Milton Lomask, *Exploration* (Scribner, 1988), p. 38.

p. 49: "Pneumonia of right lung . . ." Dugard, pp. 80–81.

Chapter 8:

p. 54: "There is a group . . ." Livingstone, pp. 254–255.

p. 54: "You have brought me new life." Dugard, p. 270.

p. 55: "I was converted by him . . ." Judy Alter, *Extraordinary Explorers and Adventurers* (Children's Press. 2001), p. 180.

Chapter 9:

p. 61: "Nothing earthly will make me . . ." Baker, p. 360.

p. 63: "It is not all pleasure . . ." Livingstone, p. 583.

p. 65: "Brought by faithful hands . . ." Dugard, pp. 308–309.

Afterword:

p. 69: "Nowhere have I ever appeared . . ." Arnold, p. 135.

INDEX

Page numbers in **boldface** are illustrations.